TREASURES

for Two-Part Choir

Compiled and Arranged by Tom Fettke

From the

Series

Lillenas PUBLISHING COMPANY

KANSAS CITY, MO 64141

CONTENTS

All in the Name of Jesus *with*
Take the Name of Jesus with You 77

Antiphonal Praise *with*
How Great Is He 3

Arise! Shine! 70

Behold the Man 54

Come, Thou Almighty King 34

God Exalted Him 85

Great Is the Lord 96

Holy Is the Lord *with*
Come, Worship the Lord 47

In Christ Alone 10

Jesus, Lord to Me 62

Like a Lamb Who Needs the Shepherd *with*
The Lord's My Shepherd 38

Lord of All 88

Magnify the Lord 18
O Magnify the Lord
Stand Up and Bless the Lord

People Need the Lord 25

Antiphonal Praise

with

How Great Is He

Arr. by Tom Fettke

CD: 03

cresc. and accel.

ia, Al - le - lu - ia.

*"How Great Is He" (Linda Lee Johnson-Tom Fettke)

A little faster ♩ = ca. 84
Solo *mf*

How great is He, How strong and

cresc.

might - y! King of kings, Lord of

In Christ Alone

Words and Music by
SHAWN CRAIG and DON KOCH
Arr. by Tom Fettke

CD: 07

Alto optional

hand. But those tro-phies are not e-qual to the

grace _____ by which I stand. _____ In Christ a-

lone _____ I place my trust and find ___ my

CD: 08

vic - to-ry, let it be said of me, My source of strength,＿＿＿ my

source of hope＿＿＿＿ is Christ a - lone.＿＿＿＿＿＿ In ev - 'ry

source of hope＿＿＿＿ is Christ a - lone.＿＿＿

Magnify the Lord

including
O Magnify the Lord
Stand Up and Bless the Lord

Arr. by Tom Fettke

CD: 10

With excitement ♩ = ca. 104

9 *"O Magnify the Lord" (Melodie and Dick Tunney)

mag - ni - fy,___ O   mag - ni - fy___ the   Lord_____ with   me,   and
wor - ship Him,___ O   wor-ship Christ_ the   Lord_____ with   me,   and

er. King of kings and Lord of

lords, May His name be lift - ed high for -

ev - er! Stand

Alto optional

CD: 13

35 *"Stand Up and Bless the Lord" (Traditional)

22

People Need the Lord

Words and Music by
GREG NELSON and PHILL McHUGH
Arr. by Tom Fettke

32

Come, Thou Almighty King

Call to Worship

MICHAEL HUDSON

GARY DRISKELL
Arr. by Tom Fettke

Like a Lamb Who Needs the Shepherd

with

The Lord's My Shepherd

Arr. by Tom Fettke

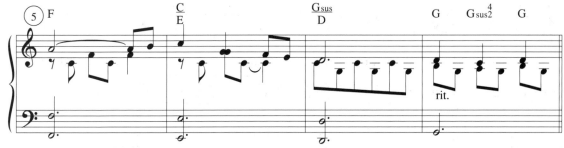

*"Like a Lamb Who Needs the Shepherd" (Ralph Carmichael)

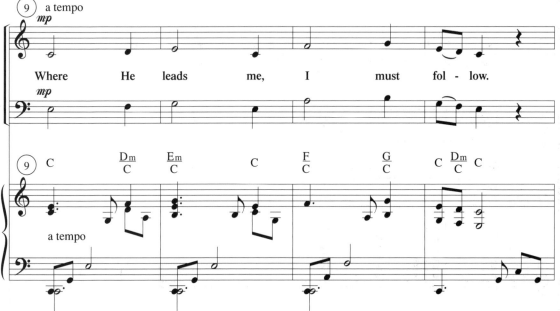

Where He leads me, I must fol - low.

Like a lamb who needs the shep - herd,

At His side I'll al - ways

stay._____ Through the night His

44

Holy Is the Lord

with

Come, Worship the Lord

Arr. by Tom Fettke

*"Come, Worship the Lord" (Twila Paris)

Come, wor-ship the Lord God Al-might-y for His lov-ing-kind-ness is ev - er-last - ing. His

Alto optional

praise,_____ Ho - ly___ is the Lord,

A sus   A   Bm7   A/C#   D   G   A/C#   D   D/C#

sub. mf

rul - ing in wis - dom and grace; Fall on your face be -

Bm   Bm/A   E/G#   E7/G#   A   F#/A#   F#7/A#   Bm   A   A/G

sub. mf

fore   Je - sus,   the   Lord   of   lords,   Righ- teous for -

D/F#   D   D/F#   E/G#   A   A/G

Behold the Man

Words and Music by
JIMMY OWENS
Arr. by Tom Fettke

know that this was God the Fa - ther's plan, Born of love to bring re-demp-tion

down to man, That in love He gave His on - ly Son so that

we might be for - giv - en. Be - hold the

Jesus, Lord to Me

Words and Music by
GARY McSPADDEN and GREG NELSON
Arr. by Tom Fettke

sun-rise when the tomb_____ was o-pened wide, Would
sun-rise

I have___ known___You, could___ I have___
Would___ I have___ known___You,

seen That You were more than just a___ man;

Arise! Shine!

Words and Music by
ROBERT STERLING and CHRIS MACHEN
Arr. by Tom Fettke

All in the Name of Jesus

with

Take the Name of Jesus with You

Arr. by Tom Fettke

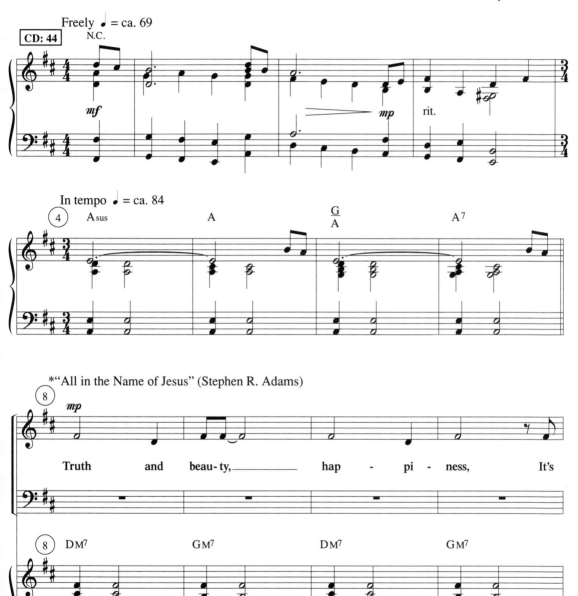

*"All in the Name of Jesus" (Stephen R. Adams)

Truth and beau-ty, _____ hap - pi - ness, It's

81

God Exalted Him

Call to Worship or Service Closer

LINDA LEE JOHNSON

TOM FETTKE
Arr. by Tom Fettke

Lord of All

Words and Music by
PHILL McHUGH
Arr. by Tom Fettke

90

al-ways been and al-ways will be Lord of_____ all.

CD: 53

Great Is the Lord

DEBORAH D. SMITH

MICHAEL W. SMITH
Arr. by Tom Fettke

Great is the Lord,___ now lift up your voice; now lift up your voice:

Great_____ is the Lord!___

_____ Great_____ is the

100